THE
PICTURE LIFE
OF
Jesse Jackson

WARREN J.
HALLIBURTON

Franklin Watts
New York/London/Toronto/Sydney/1984
Revised Edition

Cover photograph courtesy of UPI.

Photographs courtesy of AP/Wide World: pp. 4, 8, 15, 16, 20, 23, 31, 32, 35, 43; Tharpe from Monkmeyer Press Photo Service: p. 7; North Carolina Agricultural and Technical State University: pp. 11, 12 (top and bottom), 27; Greensboro News and Record: p. 19; Chester Higgins, Jr.: p. 24; Bruce Anspach/Art Resource: p. 28; Owen Franken/Sygma: pp. 36, 39; UPI: pp. 40, 44; Julia Jones, 1984: p. 46.

Library of Congress Cataloging in Publication Data
Halliburton, Warren J.
The picture life of Jesse Jackson.
Summary: Traces the life of the Afro-American minister and civil rights worker from his childhood in South Carolina through his 1984 campaign for the Democratic presidential nomination.
1. Jackson, Jesse, 1941–   —Juvenile literature.
2. Afro-Americans—Biography—Juvenile literature.
3. Civil rights workers—United States—Biography—Juvenile literature. [1. Jackson, Jesse, 1941–
2. Afro-Americans—Biography. 3. Civil rights workers]
I. Title.
E185.97.J25H3   1984   323.4′092′4 [B] [92]   84-5142
ISBN 0-531-04808-X

Second Edition
Copyright © 1972, 1984 by Franklin Watts, Inc.
Printed in the United States of America
6 5 4 3 2 1

THE
PICTURE LIFE
OF
JESSE JACKSON

If you run, you might lose. But if you don't run, you're guaranteed to lose. Run! And if you run, you might win. Run! Run for the courthouse. Run for the statehouse. Run for the White House. But run!

These were the words of Jesse Jackson. They expressed his belief in life and in himself. This faith gave him the strength to try to become the first black president of the United States.

Jesse Jackson developed his strength over many hard years. He was born in Greenville, South Carolina, October 8, 1941. His family was poor but there was lots of love. This love helped give him the strength he needed, even as a child. Because it was also in Greenville that Jesse experienced something he would never forget.

Jesse was only six years old when he learned how black people were treated. In a neighborhood store, filled with black customers, he was happy and impatient to buy candy. Jesse whistled. The white storekeeper looked at the

Jesse Jackson grew up in a time of Ku Klux Klan demonstrations.

little black child and decided to teach him a lesson. Pulling out a gun, he pointed it at Jesse. The black customers stared. None dared say a word. They were too afraid. It was this fear that Jesse could never forget.

After that incident, he began to notice black life in the South. On his five-mile hike to school each day, he passed another school—one he could not attend. It was for whites only. The school he attended was for blacks only. The men who wore uniforms, he noted, were always white. And the white police chased the black men who hung around in their old, worn-out clothes.

Until fairly recent times, black people throughout the South had to use separate public facilities, such as waiting rooms.

Jesse learned that to be black was to be different. He made up his mind. He would work hard and become somebody special.

Strong and active, Jesse grew into a star athlete. In high school he played football, basketball, and baseball. His success in sports helped to develop his confidence. He also realized what hard work could do. For his success in athletics, Jesse Jackson was awarded a scholarship to the University of Illinois.

Number 48, Jesse Jackson

J.J

But a black athlete in a white college was a lonesome person. There were few black students, and white students led lives of their own. After one year, Jesse left the college. The all-black Agricultural and Technical State University at Greensboro, North Carolina, welcomed him. Jesse became an honor student as well as an outstanding athlete.

Top: *as president of the student government at North Carolina Agricultural and Technical State University.* Bottom: *Jesse Jackson returns to his college as a guest speaker.*

Jesse also became active in the struggle to gain legal rights for black people. This happened while he was preparing a composition for one of his classes. In need of special information, he went to the public library. He was turned away. Black people, he was told, were not admitted. An angry Jesse Jackson decided to do something about this injustice. As president of the student body, he organized a sit-in.

Over 300 black students are arrested while seeking entrance to a "white-only" public cafeteria in Greensboro, North Carolina, in 1963.

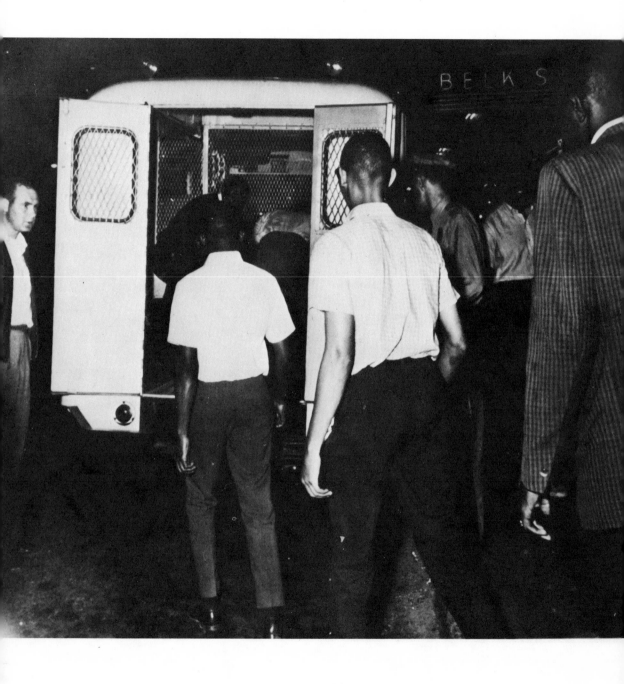

Large numbers of black students gathered, refusing to move until the library opened its doors to them. They won their fight. The library agreed to allow black people to use its books.

Students are arrested for demonstrating against segregation.

Before long, Jesse found himself leading other demonstrations. Some were sit-ins at lunch counters and others were protest marches. Their purpose was to expose the wrongs practiced against black people.

Jesse Jackson under arrest and on his way to jail

It was while demonstrating at the jail in Greensboro, North Carolina, that Jesse came to an important conclusion. When he and other young blacks sang or prayed, the white police standing by grew confused and silent. They no longer threatened attack. Jesse was never to forget that experience.

Jesse Jackson gives the clenched-fist salute from a police van after he was arrested in New York City for demonstrating against segregation.

During his senior year at North
Carolina Agricultural and Technical
State, Jesse married Jacqueline Lavinia
Brown. Continuing his studies, he
was graduated in 1964 with honors.
Then he went to work. He was
employed by the governor of the state
to work in politics. But Jesse was not
happy. For one whole year he thought
about how he could make the most of
his life. Jesse knew that it would have
to be through helping his people. He
decided the best way to do that was
to train for the ministry.

*Jesse Jackson with his family after receiving
an honorary Doctor of Divinity degree
from Chicago Theological Seminary*

Jesse Jackson finished his religious training as a minister. And he and his wife started a family. Theirs was to grow into a rewarding home life, with five children.

Relaxing at home

Meanwhile, what he had done to improve the lives of black people attracted the attention of the Reverend Martin Luther King, Jr. As president of the Southern Christian Leadership Conference (SCLC), the famous civil-rights leader asked Jesse to help him find jobs for black people. Dr. King named this assignment Operation Breadbasket.

The Reverend Martin Luther King, Jr.,
with the Reverend Jesse Jackson

SUPPORT S.C.L.C's

OPERATION
BREADBASKET
◆
FIGHT AGAINST A&P

— DEMANDS —

1. That William Kane, President of A&P meet with the Ministers of Breadbasket.

2. That a greater percentage of Blacks be employed at all levels in offices, warehouses and stores.

3. That A&P deposit monies received in Black Communities in Black Banks.

4. That Black Insurance Companies/Brokers handle insurance on A&P stores in Black Communities.

5. That Black Newspapers and Radio Stations get a fair share of A&P advertising dollars.

6. That Black Service Companies get service contracts in stores.

7. That products manufactured by Black Companies be chaired and prominently displayed in A&P stores.

8. That high quality meats and produce be sold in stores in Black Communities.

DON'T SHOP A&P

FOR INFORMATION: 799-2923

Meeting with other black ministers in Chicago in 1966, Jesse Jackson organized them into an active group. Together they made demands on white businesses. Hire blacks, they said, or go out of business. Most of these business people decided to hire blacks.

Carrying a list of Operation Breadbasket demands to the A&P.

But two years later Jesse's feelings of success were destroyed. In 1968 Martin Luther King was dead, killed by an assassin's bullet. The tragedy left Jesse with a hard choice: whether to continue in the Southern Christian Leadership Conference or to form his own organization. He decided to form his own organization, naming it Operation PUSH—People United to Serve Humanity.

Beginning in 1971, he developed Operation PUSH in fourteen cities. Not content with this achievement, Jesse

The day before Martin Luther King, Jr., was assassinated in Memphis, Tennessee. Left to right: Hosea Williams, Jesse Jackson, Dr. King, and the Reverend Ralph Abernathy.

used it to concentrate on another interest close to his heart, black pride. Using his powerful gift for public speaking, he captured large audiences of black ministers, business people, youth leaders, and anyone else he could find in the black community. As they listened, Jesse's audiences thrilled at his words and shouted encouragement. "Right on, Jesse! Tell it, brother." When Jesse finished, he cried out, "I am somebody!" And the crowd echoed, "I am somebody!" The words were a beautiful reminder to a people discovering their pride.

Jesse Jackson, in a rousing speech, announces plans to register eight million black voters.

His great success with young people led him to develop the program, PUSH-Excel. This program was designed to improve the reading skills, study habits, and general behavior of ghetto school students in Chicago. At the same time, Jesse taught them a sense of self-worth and responsibility. Participating students pledged to study two hours every night, without television, radio, or the telephone.

Students in Chicago give Jesse Jackson their signed pledges to improve in their studies.

Reverend Jackson believes this program is important not only to black children, but to America's future. Its success was rewarded with a government grant of money, and PUSH-Excel has been established in other cities.

For over twenty years, Jesse Jackson has succeeded in his efforts to increase voter registration, create jobs, and develop the pride of black people. As he turned his attention to international relations and development, black interest in politics grew.

Jesse Jackson urges black Americans to register and vote in elections.

More and more black Americans began to participate in elections. Some were elected to political office. Others began serving as volunteers. Black Americans were discovering the power of the ballot.

Realizing the potential of the black vote, Jesse Jackson announced his candidacy for president. It was not a

Left to right: *Andrew Young, former U.S. ambassador to the United Nations; Jesse Jackson; and Richard Hatcher, mayor of Gary, Indiana.*

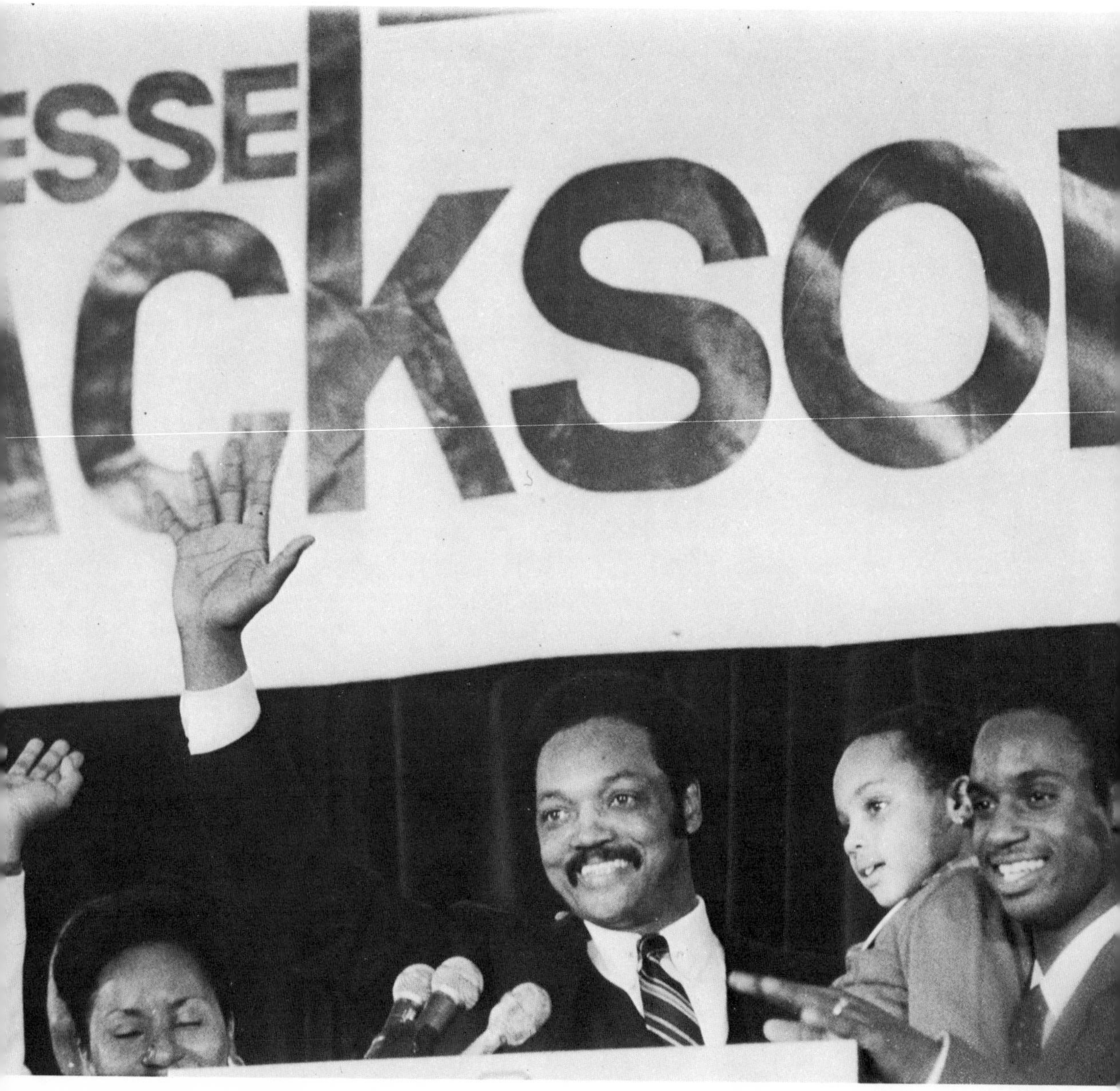
ESSE
CKSO

popular decision, even among many black Americans. Nor was it seriously considered among most white Americans. Not until a strange chain of events began to happen did these attitudes change.

The events began in early December 1983. United States troops were engaged in a peace mission in faraway Syria. Suddenly, Syrian guns fired at American aircraft. Two days later, on December 4, American aircraft were ordered to strike back. During this attack, one craft was shot down. One of

Jesse Jackson with his wife and two of their children, after announcing his candidacy for the presidency

its airmen died of injuries. The other, Lieutenant Robert O. Goodman, Jr., was captured by the Syrians.

Efforts by the United States government to free Lieutenant Goodman were hampered by the political situation. The two countries had greater issues to settle than the freedom of Lieutenant Goodman. His imprisonment dragged on into weeks.

Then came an announcement by one of the presidential candidates. Jesse Jackson was going to Syria to seek Lieutenant Goodman's release.

Jesse Jackson with Lieutenant Goodman's mother, just before his departure for Syria.

The mission was a political gamble, possibly a dangerous one. Jesse was going into an enemy country as a private citizen. He was also going without the approval of his government. America awaited the outcome in suspense.

The news broke like a bombshell. The mission was a success. Jesse Jackson was coming home with Lieutenant Goodman. He had achieved what no one else could accomplish, not even the United States government. He was welcomed home, a hero.

Lieutenant Goodman, with Jesse Jackson at his side, waves to the crowd upon his arrival in the United States.

Jesse Jackson has said that his talent is to motivate people, to get them moving and acting, in order to solve problems. He has accomplished this best by example. The promising young man chosen by Martin Luther King, Jr., to help get jobs for black people has grown into a statesman. He is more certain of himself, as others are more certain about him. He is also more determined to run, as others are to see him run—to his full potential and for the service of humanity.

ABOUT THE AUTHOR

Warren J. Halliburton, like Jesse Jackson, entered college on an athletics scholarship. After receiving a master's degree in education from Columbia University, he went on to teach at the college level in the South and later in New York City.

Mr. Halliburton is the author of *American's Color Caravan, They Had a Dream,* and *American Majorities and Minorities.* In addition, he has written numerous short stories and biographies of members of minority groups.